Book Cover by Hannah Troyer with illustration from Sir John Tenniel, 1865 edition of Alice's Adventure in Wonderland.

Tarot Card scans from CharkaGallery

ISBN 9798988209621 (paperback) | ISBN 9798227562210 (ebook)

Fonts: The Seasons, Playfair, Bell MT, Rufina, Beloved Ornamental

Published by Plush & Regal Press
www.plushandregal.press

From Hannah, with love

A JOURNEY THROUGH THE TAROT

Contents

Welcome

~~~~~~~~~~

YOU, MY DEAR ONE, ARE GETTING READY TO EMBARK ON AN EPIC JOURNEY.

A journey of self discovery, that will bring answers to some of life's toughest questions and open doors that will lead to worlds full of even more questions.

It is all a journey on the spiral— falling down the rabbit hole in an effort to make the unknown, known.

Keep in mind on your journey, that the tarot is a tool that has been used by many for centuries, as a game and as a tool to understand life— how fitting? As life itself is just a game.

This is my personal understanding of the cards. I see them as an epic story— one scene flowing into the next. I hope you enjoy this story guide. It is my hope that as your read, you may begin to think... *Curiouser and curiouser!*

The Major Arcana

THE FOOL.

The Fool

The seed of intention. The little tiny wormhole that says there must be something more to this life. The feeling right before you let yourself fall into the unknown.

You may find you can easily put yourself into the place of The Fool as he travels through the different archetypes.

Truly, this is what we are meant to do with the major arcana cards.

These 22 cards are archetypes that help us break up our life into a journey of different experiences— an exploration of distinctly different energies.

One energy leading into the next, with points where we can look back and see how far we've come.

Once we say yes to the journey, everything changes.

We are led on a spiralic voyage inward where everything looks similar, but somehow different. Maybe we feel a little like Alice in Wonderland falling down the rabbit hole.

> *"If I had a world of my own, everything would be nonsense. Nothing would be what it is, because everything would be what it isn't. And contrary wise, what is, it wouldn't be. And what it wouldn't be, it would. You see?"*
>
> *Lewis Carroll, Alice's Adventures in Wonderland*

Welcome to a world of your own, my friend.

Through this journey, you may realize that nothing is really what you had thought it to be. If you can truly let go of what you think things ought to be, you will find an exciting new world waiting on the other side of the rabbit hole.

1 The Magician

SPEAKING OF RABBITS, THE MAGICIAN IS CARD NUMBER ONE IN THE TAROT.

Here we learn what is possible.

(Spoiler alert, anything is possible.)

In this scene, you'll find representations of each of the minor arcana suits: the wands, the swords, the cups & the pentacles. Each suit represents an element: fire, air, water & earth.

The Magician is showing us that anything is possible, if we understand the elements that make up the Universe.

The magic wand in the magician's hand represents the fifth element of ether— the invisible glue that holds everything in this existence together and animates it to life.

Above the magician's head we find an infinity symbol— symbolic language for abundance.

Anything and everything is possible, as long as you understand the elements and how to manipulate them. This is called alchemy— the process of transforming matter.

It takes a high level of mastery to transform matter, but an understanding of the elements is the basis at which we all must start.

The High Priestess

AND HOW COULD WE PRACTICE ALCHEMY WITHOUT TRULY KNOWING WHAT WE WANT?

The High Priestess holds the key to our inner-standing. Balancing the yin and the yang, we begin to find our intuition— the voice deep inside, so faint at times that we could barely even call it a voice.

The High Priestess beckons us to the depths of our soul, to listen to our inner knowing.

The answers here are unexplainable with mind based logic. The mind does not understand this realm.

Here is where we learn to trust ourselves. We learn that the mind is not where to start looking for our answers.

Here we learn to indulge in the intuitive, "yes" or "no" without further explanation.

It is here where we don't second guess and we don't ask for more information. We simply follow the guidance of the inner oracle.

3 The Empress

INDULGING IN THIS INNER ORACLE WILL LEAD US FURTHER DOWN THE RABBIT HOLE OF YIN AND YANG.

The third stop on this journey is The Empress.

The divine feminine.

She just is.

She has fully accepted this inner knowing and allows herself to be held and guided by it always.

She understands that she is fully taken care of by God, and so she can allow herself to just be.

She is magnetic. She devotes herself to care taking and nurturing herself and those who are magnetized to her.

She basks in her abundance. She is in a constant state of gratitude and grace.

She has authority over herself because she trusts her intuition and she submits to the external provision and protection that she has manifested.

A Journey Through the Tarot

The Emperor

THE EMPEROR IS THE PROVIDER AND PROTECTOR. HE IS THE REASON HIS EMPRESS CAN REST EASY IN THE FIELDS OF HER ABUNDANCE.

He is the authority archetype— creating his empire through divine "yeses" and "nos".

He understands that every boundary creates a reality. Every energy he allows to penetrate the walls of his empire will change it for better or for worse.

He is always keenly aware of how energies interact, and how they will affect what he has built and is now protecting.

He knows when to say yes and when to say no and does not think twice about it.

He is in full service to his empire — to himself and to his empress.

He creates the structures, systems and boundaries that will create the foundation of all things that will grow within his domain.

5 The Hierophant

THE FIRST THING THAT MUST GROW IN ANY HEALTHY AND CONSCIOUS EMPIRE, IS A SPIRITUAL DISCIPLINE TO GIVE US TOOLS TO MASTER THE HUMAN EXPERIENCE.

The Hierophant rises to leadership as the spiritual leader. The Hierophant has learned enough on this journey to know that all the answers you need are within you.

All is created and stems from the divine intuition— the holy yes & no.

This is where the answers begin to expand. The yeses turn into practices and the no's turn into laws.

The keys to growth begin to unlock the doors to a deeper knowledge.

The mind starts to become involved as practices emerge which harness the mind into its place.

A deep knowledge of the self begins to form through conscious practice and adherence to law.

The Lovers

ONCE THE SELF MASTERY REACHES A CERTAIN LEVEL, CONSCIOUSNESS MUST BEGIN TO EXPERIENCE ITSELF OUTSIDE THE VESSEL IT CAME HERE IN.

A mirror is needed, and so The Lovers emerge.

New worlds feel like they are bursting forth through the exploration of this experience— being a soul in a body seeing itself as though in a reflection.

The energy starts to change and shift as new parts of the self are explored.

The relationship with the self deepens as the relationship with "other" blossoms.

The heavens appoint and watch over these divine matches to ensure that the reflections are as clear as possible, for the highest and greatest evolution of consciousness.

7 The Chariot

WE ARE NOW EXPERIENCING LIFE OUTSIDE THE SELF — OUTSIDE THE INNER REALMS.

As these divine matches build in intensity, we must lean on what we've already learned.

External energies culminate around us and we must learn how to harness them.

The Chariot recognizes the direction he wants to go, and utilizes these energies to help him reach his goals.

He starts to put everything in its place, so that all can be of service to his own highest good.

We are venturing out of the physical reality that we've known and learned from at this time.

We are finding new horizons as we gather speed in our chariot adorned with all the knowledge we have collected thus far.

Strength

THE JOURNEY STARTS TO FEEL CYCLICAL NOW.

We've been here before but it looks a little different.

The need for alchemy arises. We pull on wisdom teachings we learned way back with The Magician.

Strength is where we put our knowledge to the test.

Can we really rely on the elements? Does intuition really know the way? Are we really safe? Is anything really possible?

You approach your trials with a gentle compassion that calms even the rage of a lion.

Fear cannot be present when we have this level of understanding.

The tests show up and time after time you use your knowledge to alchemize the situations you find yourself in.

You watch as your knowledge turns into first hand experience.

9 The Hermit

THERE COMES A TIME WHEN YOU MUST RETURN TO YOUR CENTER.

The path becomes dim and you must light a lamp and remember the importance of being alone, for you are really all you have.

The Hermit emerges to teach the lesson of solitude—the return to the self.

You remember your first lessons about intuition and inner knowing.

You must come back into this place on a deeper, more physical level now.

Now that you are out in the world, this experience becomes more physical.

You retreat to find solace, to remember who you are.

You retreat to build the sense of self in the midst of these new challenges of life.

The Wheel of Fortune 10

AND THANK GOD YOU RETURNED HERE WHEN YOU DID, BECAUSE THE WHEEL OF FORTUNE IS SPINNING NOW AND YOU DON'T HAVE ANY IDEA WHERE IT WILL LAND.

As this wheel spins whirling different energies you've never seen before, you make your way to the center.

From your center position, you are able to be the observer as the wheel turns and you stay rooted and grounded.

You remember that you have created all of this.

You remember that you can trust that you are divinely held and guided through it all.

By now you have learned many times that all things come and go, all things blend into each other.

All is a lesson waiting to be learned and experienced.

11 Justice

You revel in the sword that brings truth and the scales that bring balance. New law is created as the new energies show themselves.

The sure yeses and nos that created your first boundaries have turned into a sharp truth and a sure balance.

The justice is harsh, but there is a higher knowledge at play. Truth is truth and justice must be served to keep all in balance as your reality rapidly expands.

Trust in this truth is key.

You have already learned the importance of boundaries which is the foundation of this system.

Justice knows just the same that different energies will create different realities, and balance must be maintained for the good of all.

The Hanged Man 12

THE HARSHNESS OF TRUTH REALLY SETS IN AS WE ENTER THE REALM OF THE HANGED MAN.

As he hangs upside down from the tree, justice is satisfied.

Although this may seem cruel and torturous, the hanged man is in full surrender and trusts in the process. The halo around his head signifies a higher knowledge.

He has a higher perspective. He allows himself to be in this position because he knows that somehow he is leading the way.

He is part of a living lesson.

The hanged man relaxes into the knowing that he understands what needs to be done, even if others don't.

He sacrifices himself for the greater expansion of consciousness as he trusts the process fully.

THE HANGED MAN.

13 Death

The rider of this white horse carries a black flag with a white rose— a symbol of purification and beauty.

The field is full of death and mourning while the sun rises in the background.

We meet ourselves yet again on a different plane. We meet death and we see ourselves in a new mirror this time.

Just as we experienced ourselves through seeing the soul of another— we now experience ourselves in death.

We look into the mirror of our soul separating from the physical body.

Who we are is dying and our attachment to the experiences we have had is dying as well.

But in every death, there is a rebirth.

Temperance

AS THE REBIRTH BEGINS, WE FIND OURSELVES BETWEEN WORLDS.

Temperance has one foot in the water, one foot on the land.

We are again ready to step into a new reality— to leave what we've known and start on another leg of the journey.

The spiral begins to bend deeper into itself.

The balance is being restored.

Heaven and earth meet and the veil between worlds is bridged.

We receive a new degree of our calling.

We have renewed strength and clarity.

We have touched heaven and are ready to return back to earth...

15 The Devil

...BUT FIRST WE MUST VISIT HELL.

We tumble from our balanced bliss down into the test that is the beginning of this next level.

We meet The Devil and are confronted with choices to make. We realize the shackles of this physical existence and must reckon with them.

There are no wrong choices here, only lessons we can choose to learn.

We look up to see the symbol of the pentagram above the Devil's head— a sign of protection from evil.

We are reminded of the trust we have leaned on that has never failed us— even when faced with our own death.

THE DEVIL .

The Tower  16

THE CHOICES WE MAKE HAVE CONSEQUENCES AND TEACH US LESSONS ABOUT THIS PHYSICAL REALITY.

Choices were made and The Tower we thought we were headed for is now crumbling to the ground before our very eyes.

The old bricks could not withstand the frequency of this new reality, and so it must fall.

As detrimental and devastating as this may seem— in the midst of the chaos, you remember your center.

You remember the things you have been through. You know that there is a grander plan at play.

You trust that this tower must come down fully in order to build up what you really want to create.

17 The Star

THE TOWER HAS CRUMBLED AND IN ITS WAKE YOU FIND YOURSELF IN THE DEPTHS OF A LIFE GIVING POOL.

The Star reveals the connection of the conscious and the subconscious.

You dive in deep to this well of knowledge. The information held in the water, the ways the stars connect, there is so much to learn in it all.

It seems never ending but you commit to being the bearer of this water.

What once felt confusing and unknown to you is beginning to make sense and take its place.

As you begin to uncover these nuggets of knowledge, you realize that this is all part of you.

This is all part of what makes you a unique and multifaceted being.

These are your gifts you have come here to offer to the world.

The Moon

THE STARS GIVE WAY TO THE MOON AS YOU IMMERSE YOURSELF FULLY IN THE ENERGY OF THE NIGHT.

Your instincts are strengthened and the practice of bearing this watery knowledge is allowing deeper and deeper truths to emerge.

You allow yourself to see how your emotions may also play into this understanding you have of truth. It feels overwhelming at times— scary even, but you trust.

You return to the deep knowing that you are safe and held as you explore.

Your emotions become a vast landscape that stretches further than you can even conceive of.

It creates realities.

19 The Sun

NIGHT TURNS TO DAY, THE SUN RISES AND THE FULL EXPRESSION OF THESE TEACHINGS IS REALIZED.

Everything becomes integrated and you can lean into the landscape that you have created.

There is a newness— an innocence to this day, as there is every time the sun sets and rises.

The grounds that you watered in the night time have now blossomed beautiful plants and flowers.

You allow yourself to be seen in your vibrancy.

You are unapologetically yourself. You bask in the sun and know that you can trust this expression.

You show yourself so that others may see that they too can live into their fullness.

Judgement 20

The beginning of the end.

The trumpets sound and all are called to reckon with themselves and God. The white flag donning a red cross is flown, a sign that cosmic order must be restored.

What lessons do you still need to learn?

What loose ends have you left untied?

Have you harbored any judgement?

Where does fear still reside in your soul?

This is your final call.

The playing field is leveled.

The angel lovingly welcomes all to come.

No matter what degree of consciousness you have attained throughout your journey, all are worthy to be called home.

21 The World

AND HOME IS WHERE YOU WILL RETURN.

The World holds all that is and all that has been.

It holds your lessons, your experiences, your truth.

The magical wands of alchemy appear again in the hands of the woman who represents the world.

The glue of ether emerges and shows itself.

We have reached the final alchemical process.

We have mastered the elements and thus mastered this level in the spiral of reality.

We may rise up now and look with a birds eye view at what we've created.

We stay here just long enough to soak in the energy, before our magic wand poofs us back down to earth.

Back down to our cliff where we began.

XXI

THE WORLD.

the Suit of Wands

The suit of Wands in the tarot takes us on a journey through the element of Fire. This suit is about our energy— our own personal fire.

We begin our journey through the minor arcana with the Wands, the Fire, as this is the element with which life begins.

In astrology, the Fire comes first. We must have the "spark of life" before anything else can be experienced.

Everything is energy and nothing exists without it.

This journey will teach you about your own energy, how to harness it, understand it and manage it.

Pay close attention to the progression and try to put yourself in the story.

How can you apply this to your own journey?

But above all— have fun!

The Ace

THE SUIT OF WANDS INTRODUCES US TO THE ELEMENT OF FIRE.

The fire that fuels our soul. Where we pour our energy.

We begin with fire because everything begins with fire— a Divine spark that starts it all.

Starting with the Ace of Wands— this card embodies the purest energy of the suit.

This Ace holds infinite possibilities— the ability to pour out your life in complete service to the highest good.

The hand of God holds out the Wand and begs, "Here, take it— it is yours."

Here is where you learn that you have access to unlimited possibilities.

The Two

IN THE TWO OF WANDS YOU WAIT PATIENTLY FOR WHAT WILL BE COMING YOUR WAY.

You've set the intention and now it is time to trust that the Universe will provide.

This is not the time for action or movement— this is the time for faith.

This is the time to hold the intention and know that the world is at your fingertips.

You are just coming off of seeing the purity of this energy and you are ready for more— ready to experience what this looks like in real life.

You are ready to see what manifests.

The Three

The Universe is already providing and now it is time to keep a vigilant watch for what the next steps will be.

You are learning the process. You are learning that your trust and strong intentions pay off.

You've gotten a taste of what this journey will look like and it is a little about trust and a lot about patience.

All in perfect timing.

Keep the faith.

The Four

FOUR OF WANDS SEES A CELEBRATION.

You have kept the faith long enough to collect yet another Wand.

Things are starting to ramp up now and the excitement is just beginning.

This time your closest friends and family start to notice your commitment & diligence, and they throw a party to celebrate with you.

You allow yourself to receive— all is part of a grander plan.

You continue to hold your intention, although now with others involved, you find yourself getting more easily distracted.

The Five

WITH FIVE OF WANDS, YOUR PARTY TURNS SOUR.

A petty argument arises and all of a sudden you find yourself pulled into a full blown fight.

It seemed to begin out of nowhere, and somewhere in your soul it feels justified.

Remember what started this— was it worth it?

Where is your energy going now? Where is your intention in all of this?

You allow yourself to experience this fully, but you keep these questions in the back of your mind.

The Six

IN SIX OF WANDS YOU HAVE EMERGED A VICTOR AND ARE RECOGNIZED BY THE COMMUNITY FOR YOUR ACCOMPLISHMENTS.

The fight is over and you feel validated.

This feels great— finally they all see how much work you have been doing!

You lead the parade.

The community follows you through the streets and you feel like you've finally "made it." Is this the moment you have been so diligently and patiently waiting for?

A wreath is placed on your wand— a symbol of celebration and recognition.

You carry it with pride.

The Seven

THE SEVEN OF WANDS IS A SHOCK AS YOU ARE FORCED TO DEFEND YOURSELF AGAINST THOSE WHO YOU THOUGHT WERE ON YOUR SIDE JUST MOMENTS AGO.

Was it something you said? Did you do something wrong?

What turned this crowd so rapidly against you?

"Is this even worth it?" You think. Swiping left and right to defend yourself, you remember your intention, your purpose.

You had almost forgotten.

"Is *that* even worth it?" You ask.

The Eight

YOU ARE CATAPULTED FORWARD IN EIGHT OF WANDS.

It's almost too fast for words or thoughts.

One moment you are riding high, the next you are defending yourself at all costs.

Now, you're not sure where you even are.

At the very same moment you brought yourself back to your intention, you found yourself quantum leaping through time— space.

So much has happened since those beginning moments— it seemed so begrudgingly slow then.

Now, you can barely keep up.

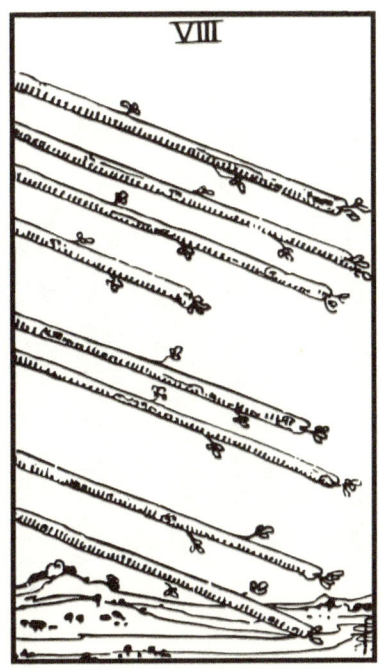

The Nine

WHEN YOU LAND AT THE NINE OF WANDS— YOU IMMEDIATELY BUILD YOURSELF A WALL.

The fear of where you've been takes over.

You don't know if the others will be coming for you. You are battered, bruised and tired.

You still hold your intention, but now with so much more baggage.

It no longer looks the same as when you began, what does it all mean?

At least behind this wall, you get to spend some time in solitude.

A Journey Through the Tarot

The Ten

AFTER MUCH CONTEMPLATION, THE TEN OF WANDS CARRIES YOU BACK HOME.

Your burden is heavy— too heavy for just you.

You have realized that you cannot carry this weight on your own. Although you were the manifestor of all of this, you recognize it is not all just for you.

You have a community you can share with, and maybe it only seems like they turned on you because you lost your own way.

Now you must share, or you will break under the weight of your own capabilities.

It's time to put down your pride, be grateful and let go.

The Page

THE PAGE OF WANDS IS OUR CURIOUS CHILD.

He plays pretend in his dress up hat. He dreams of one day ruling his own kingdom.

His dreams have no boundaries.

The potential is there but the experience is yet to come.

The ideas abound but nothing has manifested into real life quite yet.

He is still just a child and his imagination— possibly one of the most powerful forces on the planet.

A Journey Through the Tarot

The Knight

THE KNIGHT OF WANDS IS READY FOR ACTION.

He's learned what to do, read all the books and trained for this day
Now he's off to see what he can do.

The fire under him is strong and motivates him towards his goals.

He has an unquenchable thirst for success.

He has put his childhood dreams into motion, and he cannot wait to
see where it takes him.

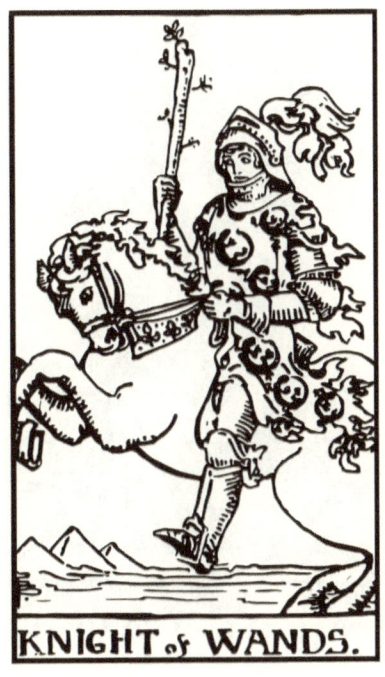

KNIGHT of WANDS.

The Queen

THE QUEEN OF WANDS BALANCES MANY THINGS AT ONCE.

She knows her power, and the powers of those around her. She has become a master of keeping things steady.

Her capacity is expanded so that she can hold many things at once. Her equilibrium allows much to be accomplished.

She has learned what it means to have balance within herself, so now she leads with that same energy.

She understands— as above, so below.

The King

THE KING OF WANDS HAS BEEN THROUGH MANY BATTLES.

He understands many things that others do not, and so his reign is simple and straightforward.

He is a master of the element of Fire— he respects it and rules accordingly.

He sees beyond what others see and keeps the peace with a strong and swift hand.

He is in complete service to others, as he knows that is the only true path to success.

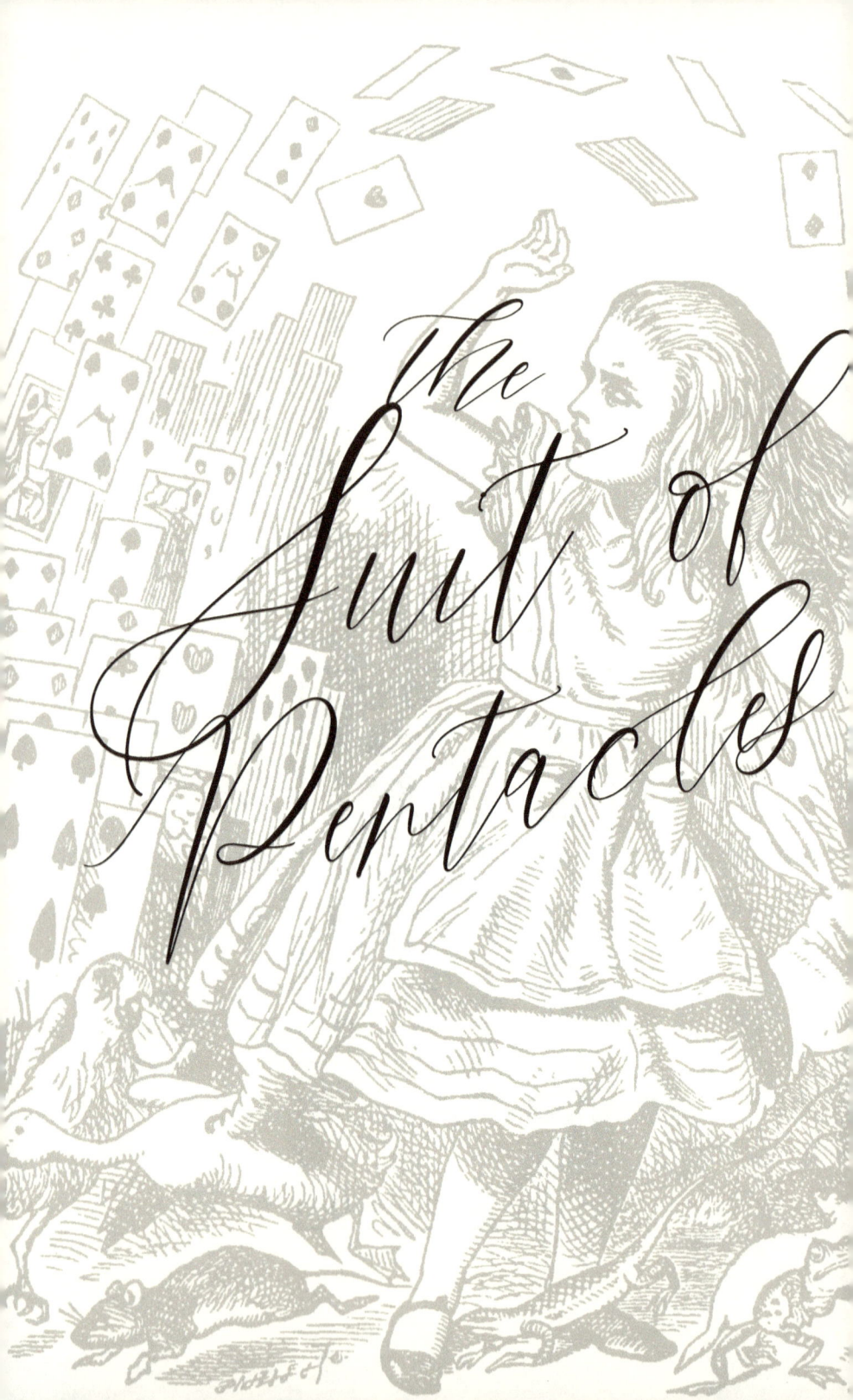

the Suit of Pentacles

⊱

WELCOME TO YOUR JOURNEY THROUGH THE PENTACLES.

The suit of Pentacles in the tarot takes us on a journey through the element of Earth.

This suit is about our physical experience— the body, the earth & the resources that we find here.

We have gone through the journey of energy and created a physical reality with it.

Now with the Pentacles, it's time to interact with the physical.

There is much to explore here.

You will learn about abundance, creating what you want and learning how to balance it.

Continue to place yourself inside the story. When have you experienced some of these same energies?

Have fun as you continue to follow the white rabbit on this journey through wonderland.

⚘

The Ace

WE MOVE FROM WANDS INTO THE NEXT SUIT, THE ELEMENT OF EARTH, THE PENTACLES.

The Pentacles represent our experience of earthly elements— resources, finances, our physical body and the like.

The journey starts as always with the Ace of Pentacles, representing the element in its purest form.

The Ace teaches what this journey will be all about— finding the key that unlocks the frequency of abundance.

The Universe hands you a giant coin symbolizing your access to this abundance, if you only would learn to accept it.

The Two

YOUR NEXT LESSON IS ABOUT BALANCE WITH THE TWO OF PENTACLES.

Here you experience that you must first achieve balance with what you have before you are able to gain anything more.

Balance is often a juggling act. It can take time and patience.

Perfecting the balance and practicing gratitude & respect for your small lot will prepare you for moving forward and stewarding more in the future.

The Three

WITH THREE OF PENTACLES, YOU MOVE INTO TEAMWORK WHERE YOU FIND YOUR TRUSTED COLLABORATORS.

You learn that you cannot do this alone, and so you must find supporters who trust what you have and are willing to work with you.

Conversely, you must learn to trust what you have and be open enough to share that with others.

Discernment also comes into play here— who is a good fit for you?

It won't be just anyone.

The Four

IN FOUR OF PENTACLES YOUR WEALTH HAS GROWN AND YOU ARE RETURNING TO THE LESSON OF BALANCE ONCE AGAIN.

This time though, you are learning to create some stability with this wealth.

You are not just juggling, but building.

Here you create systems and structures that will support you and also help your abundance to continue to grow.

You must be careful to not hold on too tightly though.

The Five

AS YOU REACH FIVE OF PENTACLES, YOU HIT A BIG LOSS.

What you've created thus far has vanished and you find yourself lost and feeling very destitute.

At least you are not completely alone.

You get caught in your own suffering here.

You are asking, "Why me?" and "What did I do to deserve this?"

You hardly even notice the sign in the window above you that is miraculously lighting your way.

A Journey Through the Tarot

The Six

IN SIX OF PENTACLES YOU HAVE FOUND ABUNDANCE AGAIN.

Here you learn to give and receive.

You know what it is to have and you know what it is to have not.

The concept of charity is introduced— the give & take.

As you experience this new idea of give & take, you are reminded again of your first teachings on balance.

Balance must always be maintained to create success.

The Seven

NOW AT SEVEN OF PENTACLES YOU SEE SOME OF THE SEEDS YOU PLANTED EARLY ON FINALLY BEGINNING TO BLOOM.

The winter has been hard but the harvest will be sweet.

It's time to learn how to reflect and give thanks for all you are receiving.

There is much work to be done but taking a moment to pause and be grateful is just as important as the work.

You learn by observing.

The Eight

IN EIGHT OF PENTACLES YOU GET BUSY WORKING.

The system you set up is working well now and there are plenty of things to get done.

You grab your tools and get to work.

Although it could seem tedious and time consuming, this too is an important part of the process.

Even when it feels tiring, overwhelming or even boring— be faithful to the work and the return shall be great.

The Nine

AT NINE OF PENTACLES YOU CAN FINALLY RELAX.

Your work, trust and dedication has paid off and you find yourself in a beautiful garden.

You can put your tools down, drop your shoulders and soften your gaze.

The harvest has been plentiful.

It's time to bask in the fruits of your labor. Enjoy your time here, you had to learn & experience much to make it this far.

The Ten

You have worked hard and been prosperous.

You've enjoyed the fruits of your labor and now it's time to pass on what you've learned & accomplished.

What will you leave behind from what you have achieved?

What seed will your work plant in the garden of those who will come after you?

You can be confident that your wisdom and resources will not stop here, but carry on in new ways for generations to come.

The Page

Opportunities abound but time is needed to see which seeds will sprout and what they will sprout into.

This little lad is awestruck by the mystery wonder of the Earth— how planting, watering, sunlight & tending might make a tiny seed grow into a giant tree.

His innocence is the fertilizer for the seeds he plants.

The Knight

THE KNIGHT OF PENTACLES IS READY TO SEE WHAT IS NOW SPROUTING IN HIS FIELD.

He takes it slow— carefully inspecting each plant as it begins to grow.

Picking out only the best specimens, he decides where he will put his energy for the best future yields.

You'll find many knights racing towards something they want, but not this knight.

He cautiously examines his environment and moves with careful intention.

The Queen

THE QUEEN OF PENTACLES GATHERS AROUND ALL HER ABUNDANCE.

She trusts that more will always flow if she maintains the balance of giving and receiving.

She takes her role very seriously by understanding and respecting the responsibility that she holds.

She takes care of all who are in need while also caring for herself.

She embodies the systems of the nature around her.

The King

THE KING OF PENTACLES IS READY TO LEAD AND TAKE AUTHORITY OVER ALL THAT COMES INTO HIS KINGDOM.

He has studied the flow of abundance and can now create what he wants or needs at will.

He uses his gifts for the good of all in his community and he understands the power his knowledge holds.

He is dependable and generous with his gifts.

He has mastered the balance.

the Suit of Swords

WELCOME TO YOUR JOURNEY THROUGH THE SWORDS.

The suit of Swords in the tarot takes us on a journey through the element of Air.

This suit is about our thinking mind, information, ideas and ultimately— truth.

We have gone through the journey of Fire & Earth with the Wands & Pentacles. Now we enter the realms of Air with Swords.

Many find this the most difficult suit to journey through.

You will learn about truth, choices and trauma.

Keep placing yourself inside of this story, even when it might be painful to remember.

Even through the difficulty, you can still find fun and whimsy— and ultimately a solid sense of truth.

The Ace

FROM PENTACLES, WE MOVE TO SWORDS— THE ELEMENT OF AIR.

The Air element teaches us about our thoughts, our mind and the way information moves.

The Ace of Swords starts you off by showing what it's like to be centered into unshakable truth.

What would it be like to never have to overthink?

What would it feel like to never be unsure of a decision on your path? To know with unwavering certainty that you were fully in truth?

This realization is what the Ace shows you that you have access to.

This is where your journey opens up.

The Two

THE TWO OF SWORDS ILLUMINATES RIGHT OFF THE BAT THAT THERE IS A DECISION TO MAKE.

Once you get a glimpse of this all knowing truth, you must now decide which way you will go.

This decision can feel like a bit of a shot in the dark, but that's just the lesson— you learn here that you don't need to "see" to make a decision.

You just need to *know*.

The Three

YOU'VE MADE YOUR DECISION, AND IT'S LED YOU INTO SOME PAIN WITH THE THREE OF SWORDS.

You're afraid if you keep going, you might end up hurt further just like you have before.

Old wounds are opening and your tendency is to harden, but it's too late— the swords have already pierced your heart.

The only thing to do now is surrender & soften.

Trust that you can continue on, even through the pain.

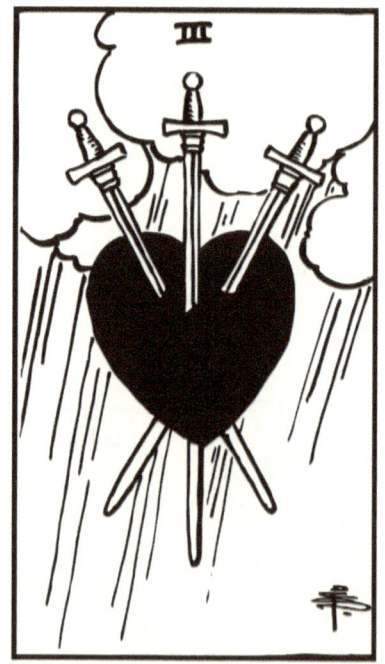

A Journey Through the Tarot

The Four

THE PAIN IS SUBSIDING BUT AS YOU MOVE INTO THE FOUR OF SWORDS YOU STILL CAN'T GET IT OUT OF YOUR MIND.

The physical pain is no longer there but it seems your mind is creating it over and over again.

Your old traumas are resurfacing and you remember all the times you've failed or been hurt before.

You display these swords and begin to even believe they could be your identity.

Yet, the truth still echoes in your mind— there is something deeper, something more.

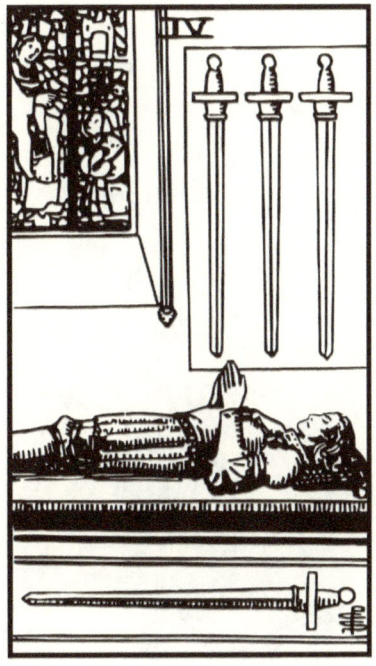

The Five

YOU TRY TO DISTRACT YOURSELF— MAYBE SOCIALIZING WILL HELP.

But as you enter the Five of Swords it only makes matters worse.

You feel triggered by others around you and you may even lash out to try getting what you want.

You hardly recognize yourself. Why are you acting this way?

You realize ultimately that others are triggering the things you must take responsibility for within yourself.

The Six

THE SIX OF SWORDS FINDS YOU LEAVING— PHYSICALLY OR POSSIBLY JUST MENTALLY.

You can no longer be around those who trigger your wounds constantly.

It's time to move on— you know too much now.

You are on a different path and it's become apparent you need a new start.

You book your one way ticket out.

Maybe this will finally be enough to end this cycle you've been stuck in.

The Seven

YOU GET WHERE YOU'RE GOING BUT THE SEVEN OF SWORDS MEETS YOU WITH MANIPULATION AND TRICKERY.

The games you play on your own mind are now meeting you in the flesh.

You might be in a new environment, but the old tricks don't work any longer.

You are too far along this journey.

You must take responsibility for this truth you say you are following, or you will be stuck in the loop of triggers and mind games forever.

The Eight

THINGS HAVE GONE TOO FAR, AND YOU ARE TRAPPED.

The Eight of Swords is illuminating these ways of thinking that you have bound yourself to.

What is it you are unable to give up? What is keeping you stuck that you are unwilling to look at?

What do you need to take responsibility for, that you've been blaming on something outside yourself?

When you finally let it go, the chains fall & you are free.

The Nine

THE DARK NIGHT OF THE SOUL COMES IN THE NINE OF SWORDS.

You've allowed yourself to be unbound, but now you must fully release what has been haunting you.

The idea of living without this pain, ironically feels unbearable.

You are afraid, maybe ultimately of yourself.

This is a reckoning with the shadow side.

The Ten

FINALLY, YOU GIVE UP ALL YOU'VE BEEN HOLDING ON TO.

The Ten of Swords finds you face down— fully surrendered.

You've faced your biggest fear. You realized it wasn't actually as scary as it seemed.

Yes, it hurt, but carrying it all hurt more.

Finally, you've made peace with what you've been fighting so long— yourself.

You've integrated your shadow.

You have found the truth.

The Page

THE PAGE OF SWORDS DREAMS OF THE DAY HE'LL GET TO TAKE HIS SWORD INTO BATTLE.

He uses his imagination to begin creating a reality he can live into.

He is learning and growing and there won't be anyone who can tell him what he can or can't do.

He knows his truth, he just might not be able to put it into words yet.

The Knight

THE KNIGHT OF SWORDS HAS FINALLY REACHED THE DAY THAT HE DREAMED OF AND IS RUSHING INTO BATTLE.

He has learned enough to set him on his way.

Now it's time for him to see what it's really like out there.

Imagination has turned to his reality. He is eager to fight for what he believes in— a true warrior for truth & justice.

He is full speed ahead and no one can stop him.

The Queen

THE QUEEN OF SWORDS KEEPS HER COMPOSURE AS SHE MOVES THROUGH HER DAILY ACTIVITIES.

Those who come to her are seeking truth and it is truth they will get— no matter if they are ready to hear it or not.

She doesn't mind being the bearer of bad news if she has to.

She knows that commitment to truth is more important than being liked.

A Journey Through the Tarot

The King

THE KING OF SWORDS IS TRUE TO HIS WORD.

His truth may anger some but he always speaks the exact words they need to hear.

He has a birds eye view from his throne on a hill & has the best interest of others in mind, always.

He has dedicated his life to seeking the truth and is practiced in communicating it.

the Suit of Cups

～

WELCOME TO YOUR JOURNEY THROUGH THE CUPS.

The suit of Cups is the final suit on our tarot journey.

The Cups take us on a journey through the element of Water.

Here we learn about emotions, feelings, creativity and love.

We have gone through the lessons of Fire, Earth & Air.

Lastly, we embark on our final journey through Water.

Water holds the final lesson— the last piece of this alchemical journey.

You will learn about peace, healing, loss and love.

As you place yourself in this story, allow yourself to not just think about but feel into the energies.

You have come so far— now it's time to learn how to let love in.

✂

The Ace

AFTER LEARNING THE LESSONS OF SWORDS, WE FINALLY REACH THE CUPS.

The Cups represent the element of Water & teach us about our emotions, our feelings and our creativity.

This overflow is palpable with the Ace of Cups.

You feel this overflow of love and peace in your whole body— unexplainable with words but somehow more expansive.

This is the gift that is always available. Your cup can always be overflowing if only you remove what is blocking the flow.

The Two

YOU GET READY FOR THIS JOURNEY WITH THE TWO OF CUPS.

Meeting the self in the other— encountering what balance feels like.

You experience what unconditional love feels like here on earth.

You connect to love by meeting it in the flesh.

"Where two or more are gathered..."

The healing begins here.

The Three

THE EXPERIENCE CONTINUES WHEN YOU ADD ANOTHER CUP WITH THREE OF CUPS.

The feeling of love, peace & flow is now experienced within a group.

You've found your support here on this earth plane and you're learning how to allow the love to expand and flow more effortlessly.

It feels like life could always be this care-free and easy.

The Four

BUT AS YOUR CAPACITY EXPANDS, FOUR OF CUPS FINDS YOU DISPLEASED
WITH HOW THINGS ARE GOING.

Your friends are gone and you're unhappy with just the three cups
you have collected thus far.

You wish for more, but can only focus on what you don't have, instead
of being grateful for what you do.

If only you could change your perspective and see that what you
desire is actually right under your nose.

The Five

THIS FEELING DEEPENS WITH THE FIVE OF CUPS AS THE CUPS YOU DID HAVE, ARE NOW ALL SPILLED OUT.

You mourn the loss of what you had and wonder how you'll ever get it back.

Deep sorrow washes over you and you feel stuck.

You still don't see what's right behind you though— now two full cups, untouched, unnoticed, just waiting to be picked up.

The Six

DEEP IN REFLECTION AFTER THIS LOSS, YOU FIND YOUR MIND WANDERING OFF.

In Six of Cups you remember your childhood, what made you happy when you were a kid.

What a simple time!

You had not yet experienced this level of grief.

Through tears you reconnect to your inner child and listen to what she has to share with you.

The Seven

MIND STILL WANDERING, YOU LAND AT SEVEN OF CUPS.

The fog is thick here and you aren't sure which way to go.

So many thoughts & feelings— you feel overwhelmed here.

You have a sense that you're starting to get somewhere, but you don't yet know where.

Lots of possibilities are opening up, but you can't seem to discern what direction to go.

Regardless, you know you can't stay stuck here any longer.

The Eight

YOU COME BACK TO REALITY IN EIGHT OF CUPS WHERE YOU FINALLY SEE YOUR PATH AGAIN.

You needed to pause and process all your feelings deeply before knowing which way to move.

Now with more cups than ever, you ironically decide to leave them all behind.

Your internal journey has taught you to trust that the path you are on will provide all you need.

The Nine

YOU ARRIVE AT THE NINE OF CUPS AND IT'S TRUE, YOU HAVE BEEN PROVIDED FOR AND THEN SOME.

You reflect once more and count your blessings here.

You are overwhelmed again but this time with gratitude.

The journey did not always feel good but it's all been worth it.

The Ten

You could not always see that this was where you were headed, but you knew the feeling you were searching for.

This is it.

You celebrate with a rainbow at the end of your journey— your friends & family have found their way back to you.

You allow yourself to receive this love fully.

The Page

THE PAGE OF CUPS IS LOST IN WONDERLAND.

He plays make believe and creates fun and freedom out of thin air.

He embodies the epitome of creativity.

He talks with his little pet fish, unafraid of if he looks silly or not.

He is having fun and that is all that matters!

The Knight

THE KNIGHT OF CUPS IS ALL GROWN UP AND HEADING OUT ON HIS MISSION.

He knows that to be successful, he must be true to himself.

With his inner child at the forefront, he moves with ease and grace.

He wears his heart on his sleeve and moves into the world with confidence in his unique gifts.

The Queen

THE QUEEN OF CUPS SPENDS HER DAYS CREATING FROM THE DEPTHS OF HER SOUL.

She is unafraid of the deep wells of her emotions as she knows that is where her creative forces come from.

She proves her skill by proudly displaying her intricate chalice that holds the holy waters.

She is a master of the inner life and she helps to guide others through their own stormy seas.

The King

THE KING OF CUPS LEADS WITH A SOFT YET STRONG POWER.

He has been through many trials of his own and explored his own inner life enough to know how to have authority over his feelings.

He keeps his inner child centered, always.

He respects the flow and is able to gratefully ride the waves as they come.

The End

⁊⁊⁊⁊⁊⁊

IT SEEMS LIKE YESTERDAY AND ALSO 10,000 YEARS AGO SINCE WE HAVE BEEN HERE.

As Alice says:

> "I wonder if I've been changed in the night. Let me think. Was I the same when I got up this morning? I almost think I can remember feeling a little different. But if I'm not the same, the next question is 'Who in the world am I?' Ah, that's the great puzzle!"

> *Lewis Carroll, Alice's Adventures in Wonderland*

And so it goes. and goes. and goes.

About the Author

Hannah is an akashic records channel, energy work practitioner & lover of esoteric knowledge. Her mission is to help souls awaken to their true spiritual nature so that they can fulfill their purpose in this lifetime.

She currently lives in Dover, Ohio with her boyfriend, Will, lots of crystals and her black lab, Luna.

Work with her on your spiritual journey at www.radiantway.net/ and follow her on Instagram: www.instagram.com/a.radiant.way

About the Publisher

Plush & Regal Press was founded in 2024 by Jessika Raisor and Trent Lindsey. They are a micro-press focused on fostering creative communities and publishing genre-bending and niche works.

They post open calls for authors on their Instagram at www.instagram.com/plushandregal

You can subscribe to their newsletter to receive monthly book recommendations from other subscribers as well as author interviews, publishing tips, and special deals.

www.plushandregal.press